APOLOGY FOR WANT

The Katharine Bakeless Nason Literary Publication Prizes

The Bakeless Literary Publication Prizes are sponsored by the Bread Loaf Writers' Conference of Middlebury College to support the publication of first books. The manuscripts are selected through an open competition and are published by University Press of New England/ Middlebury College Press.

1996 Competition Winners

Poetry
Mary Jo Bang, *Apology for Want*
JUDGE: Edward Hirsch

Fiction
Katherine L. Hester, *Eggs for Young America*
JUDGE: Francine Prose

APOLOGY FOR WANT

Mary Jo Bang

A Middlebury / Bread Loaf Book

PUBLISHED BY UNIVERSITY PRESS OF NEW ENGLAND

HANOVER AND LONDON

Middlebury College Press

Published by University Press of New England, Hanover, NH 03755

© 1997 by Mary Jo Bang

All rights reserved

Printed in the United States of America

5 4 3 2

CIP data appear at the end of the book

Acknowledgments:

Grateful acknowledgment is made to the editors of the following publications:
Colorado Review: "Nonesuch," "In This Business of Touch and Be Touched,"
"Reign of Unreason"; *Denver Quarterly:* "The Oracle"; *The Gettysburg Review:*
"Renunciation of Dreams and Such"; *Indiana Review:* "How to Leave a Prairie";
The Journal: "Where Snow Falls," "Real Time"; *The Nation:* "Gretel," "Waking in
Antibes," "Pilgrimage"; *New American Writing:* "What Was Seen," "The Desert on
Hand"; *The Paris Review:* "& There He Kept Her Very Well," "Electra Dreams,"
"If Wishes Were Horses," "No Talking"; *Partisan Review:* "Chicago"; *Salmagundi:*
"From a New Place"; *Shenandoah:* "Elegy"; *Southwest Review:* "Granite City,
Montana"; and *Witness:* "Café Edgar." "Where Snow Falls" was reprinted in the
1995/1996 Anthology of Magazine Verse & Yearbook of American Poetry.

Thanks to the many who read and commented on these poems. Especially to
Lucie Brock-Broido. And Timothy Donnelly. And forever to Edward Hirsch.

"Pilgrimage" is dedicated to Karen Kreutzinger.
"A Goddess Shakes Spring Awake" is for Timothy Donnelly.
"Like Spiders, Step by Step" is for Kymberly Taylor.
"How to Leave a Prairie" is for Susan Lee Smith.
"From a New Place" is for Catherine Sherer.
"Twilight Amnesia" is for Gary R. Bang, Jr.

for Michael *and* Rusty

and Gary

CONTENTS

WAKING IN ANTIBES

The sea dazes itself at our feet while we break
open rocks, hoping for fossil: the father

old as a trilobite; a scorpion mother with hairy legs.
Wherever we go, the sea follows. We climb hills

and find it in the distance—a tangle of tinsel,
an old absence. We read in the paper that a baby

in Northern India has been born with a long nose,
no upper lip, and two protruding teeth.

There are those who believe he is Ganesha,
the elephant-head Hindu God. Later in a museum

we walk by paintings where angel heads float,
dovewinged, above a green-faced Madonna.

Below are lakes the size of doll-house mirrors.
And as always, the Virgin is inexplicably blond.

Tomorrow we'll return to what is ours, the graffiti
we know: *Nut House, Weasel, Chucky Love.*

But not before waking one last time in a room
of Fifties blond furniture and green drapes, the sea

banging incessantly, a mechanical heart.
The two of us lying in hallowed stillness, ready

to receive trays of thick coffee and steamed milk,
potted jams, blood red in the morning light.

I once saw a cemetery marker with a person's name
followed by the word, *sleeping.*

Tomorrow will arrive wearing a white dress,
dark hair, clean hands. A knock will deliver us.

We'll rise, leaving nothing behind, no dirt clods,
no mourners. The sea will be, as we left it.

THE DESERT ON HAND

Love is also fragment: the cheek
of the moon's fat-boy face giving itself up
to be kissed,

the ingredient phrase, *I can't*
live without you, the sum of the few words
that truly invent themselves—*You are.*

Crossing the desert on hand,
there is always another to cross.
Fourteen floors above a dance band,

the lake outside the window
cooling after an all-day bake, I fell in
with one who was faint to begin.

This day is inadequate too, and tomorrow
getting shorter, even as we speak.
In this flinty age of materialism

we've grown fond of witches—
they embody our wish to believe,
to immerse ourselves

eat loaves made from wheat privily stolen
drink from cups
bearing filched wine.

To be *welcomed* into imprudence,
the elevated
tor, unbreakable oath.

PILGRIMAGE

for Karen

I wonder what you would think
of this place. Did Catholic girlhood

prepare you for a Basilica that glows
eerie white above shops selling trinkets?

On postcards, St. Therese's eyes glitter
like fool's gold. Her hair behind glass

is woven with fake flowers. And glass
holds the bones of her right forearm.

Narcissism still moves us.
Days here are fringed with sameness,

racks of dottering candles. The saint
doesn't stir on her bed of green velvet.

Where are those things we once wanted?
Fat roses in the Bishop's garden, a child

sleeping in a rented car, two girls bent
in half by pangs of laughter, all speak

garbled. Heretics believe there's a forest
not far from here—a lit clearing

where you enter, hair tied in braids
embrace a witch who smells of ginger

and cinders. Mother, you say, and she
daughters you, fattens you with longing,

restores you to what you once hoped to be:
streamer of pink cloud trailing a burst

of fireworks. (Brittle you were, yes,
but so lovely.)

REAL TIME

Made of brown Bakelite, this clock is different:
it speaks. The soft yellow face sputters
like frying bacon. Instead of an elegant *tick-tick-tick*

there's intermittent talk—firm denial of rumor
couched in a message. It insists
its occupation is unimportant:

neither dripping faucet nor ocean's teapot
of eroding waves. Time from this clock quite simply
slips over an edge

like the breakfast egg from a hot pan
that lands gently on a leaf of buttered toast.
Today, I'm less than a murmur

barely more than a hum. Clock doesn't care
where I'm going, skidding bruised on cracked ice.
Only wants to know where I've been,

with whom I spent the endless nights. Begs me to name
the beating heart, in the tigerwood box just next to it.

THE ORACLE

I listen to warnings. A distant ping may be an avalanche
or the sputter of a kitchen fire. At fourteen

I ignored sound; it was a matter of courage.
Only to regret the melted linoleum, charred paint,

mother's quiet disapproval, vague disbelief. Such lessons
make their mark. I developed a sixth sense, learned to see

without looking: the funnel cloud on the horizon,
the blue bedroom eyes of Humbert Humbert

following from the bus stop. Now I predict the future
merely by listening to echoes. A slamming door

can tell you everything you need to know. It's not a trick
only a simple matter of wisdom, an obsessive attention

to dreams. As when you dream the faint chewing of locusts
and hear the rock that signals the landslide.

You know what will happen.
You'll abandon the crops, repair the mountain again.

GRANITE CITY, MONTANA

A ghost town begs you to stare—
empty stone foundations, bleak clapboard

blown off years ago, perhaps gone
to better use: to dust covering mountain

and mine, or a layer of bedrock
for the gullied road that rises straight up

from Philipsburg. Granite hugging granite
its passion spent, landscape

of fretted rock bristling with lichen
grown ripe on pure air and indolence.

The glare of an electric bulb echoes
the barren future: nights of cold bed sheets

camouflaged in the wax and wane
of corrugated tin. And still captive

in the bulb's wavering halo, miner ghosts
of the men who rode empty ore buckets

down the mountain on Saturday nights
to be reborn in the dishevelled bed

of a tent city bordello. My bare legs graze
thorned scrub brush. The branches

hold tight imperfect berries—droplets
poised over dark earth,

brighter blood, belated warning: *It is over.*

APOLOGY FOR WANT

I've worried far too much about the eye
of the other: the shopkeeper and his lackey clerks
who think I steal.
I know I stand far too long, gazing

with wistful face at the muted tints of objects
on shelves. How smart we are all getting.
Soon we will understand everything:
why our first breath, when our last.

Why a rat, even though shocked
every time it eats, never stops knowing hunger.
How hollow-boned birds and gilled fish
estimate the size of a bounty, remember

where they stored food. There are few ways
to free the body from desire, all end in anarchy.
Tomorrow, I'll go back to the shop—the story
where it left off—

focus on those items that have bits of lavender
hidden within: gimmaled broccoli tips,
overwrought asparagus. Survival lies in resistance,
in the undersides of the leafed and delicate.

Among animals, we're the aberration:
want appropriates us,
sends us out dressed in ragged tulle, but won't tell
where it last buried the acorn or bone.

CHICAGO

On the 44th floor, plate glass against night
twins the room, invites me out
for a moment of vertigo—

a mock suicide. Below is Rush Street:
bar talk and head lamps crawl
on a lighted screen like drosophila waking

from an ether sleep. Under the bed
red coral carpet, azalea swirls.
Image is invincible, defies gravity

gets away with the breathless life of a jar.
From this leased remove, cars appear docile,
doormen surrendering. An ambulance blinks

hush and hollow. Above them, static as air
I am unfallen. The world without me
has rarely seemed this clear.

ELEGY

The eye isn't everything:
deep in the aura of a migraine
some see *de novo*

fretted fingers, tumbling knives,
the angular spectrum of eagle wings
hovering at the ceiling.

Of course there are those visions that persist:
I can still picture the voice of a once-loved—
the untrue-green of machine oil,

clarity of noon through new leaves.
And I'm sure you've seen a tree trunk
take a fence for its own

in the netherworld of objects.
Twice I took a life: first, a mouse.
Then, the cat.

In that case, no blood but a weight
more sodden than wet. Lids closed.
Always simple negation:

the astonished *Let be* disappearing
into knotgrass and bindweed,
eddy and ash.

GRETEL

Mother, I am bare in a mist-mad forest.
Only the moon shows me love.

Winter will crush me: tiny arms, pale feet,
tongue of rust. I have a thousand visions:

you ironing an enormous dress; eating
chocolate and honey, sausage

and a luscious peach; the sun drunk
and easy; spring blowing raw sky

and storm scream; someone running.
You cry, *Go, go. Take them, will you?*

He does, along the sea road with its
stopped ship fast asleep. In this place

of elaborate beauty, it is late autumn
and mostly quiet, except when

the heaven-born wind wags and flaps
the branch he left tied

to a sere white ash. Silence itself is strategy,
a signed language,

gorgeous, fluid in the hands
of those who learned it in childhood.

You know we were never meant
to live here, only to learn *relinquished,*

forsworn, to grasp with wet hands the cold
metal of life, then find a way to let go.

A SCREEN DOOR SLAMS

We leave my brother's red toy tractor
parked on the scorched lawn,
climb the hill, peer through the brush

at the forbidden: railroad tracks and hobo jungle.
We lose sight of the ravine,
the fat black snake

that falls to the bottom of every yard.
It's Friday night
fish-fry at the Fire Department.

Grown-ups drink beer from tiny metal buckets.
My sister pulls a tin fish from a metal washtub.
Off to one side,

a girl with Down's Syndrome, six years old,
lists in a wheelchair.
The mother's gray hair is drawn away

from her tight, misfortuned face.
She bends over the daughter, murmuring
into a lap robe, wiping a drool.

Rolling head, slack jaw, protruding tongue.
An immaculate blue dress,
pristine collar edged with a row of white lace.

Don't stare, my mother says. And I
the same age, air tinged
with the scent of fish and Crisco,

press my face into the ironed-cotton smell
of my mother's skirt,
whisper, *I wasn't.*

IN ORDER NOT TO BE ETEN
NOR ALL TO TORNE

The elevator mirror tells me nothing, not how
nor why—won't even say whether I'm ready.
Quiet also are the wolves

attached to my shirt cuffs and coat hem.
No trace of a howl, their canines sewn silent
through cloth. What is sound

but music of forest storm and sea spray?
Pitiable low under sentence of death.
Come here, little kitty, come here

from two boys at the well—one
with a mud streaked face. The audible wish
for unparalleled happiness. What is vision

but rheotrope and ruffle
of silver wolf-willow leaves? Trembling lambs,
some thick and short, some long and swift.

Framed face in the bevel-edge
mirror, wolf's snout hung at my neck
so no witch will hurt me. And what is harm?

Wolf-trees of morning—their children dressed
in bright green. Taking more than their share
of space, leafed heads buckling the sky above.

They restrict their neighbor's portion,
push them aside. *They must be held*—but surely
you know this—*by their ears.*

II

THE FIRST ROOM IS A WOMAN

Stethoscope in my coat pocket—a coiled snake—
I am here with Hippocrates.
Down a hall of waiting beds—mattresses ready.

The first room is a woman: mid-thirties,
hair still damp at the scalp
from tincture of iodine,

a clear drip running to the short saphenous vein
where it slips behind
the ankle's little hammer. In the room we are held

by the smell of penicillin and what drove a woman
to push a needle's bevelled edge
into the bend of her arm, *antecubital fossa,*

injecting the balm of habit and hit
until vein turned to fault line under scar
and today an abscess tense with what's done

is done. I say *You're not;* she wants to know *When?*
then *Demerol?* She surrenders her arm
to receive the scalpel's tender edge;

I slit the stretched skin,
empty the swollen pocket's curd and whey.
I'm pure reason as I pack the wound

with ribboned gauze, tucking it into the hollow
where bacteria struggled against flesh, blood.
What I cannot do

is re-work the marred surface,
rub out the rattail tracks
that map the pattern of magic's sweet distraction

over time, and time
again. She's been told before
that the leg veins would serve better;

the arm is too well-used, could even be lost.
Beginning at the dorsum of the foot,
I trace for her—by name—the tributaries

that wrap the leg, thigh.
I laud their easy access, their utility
as conduit, groove. And road.

OPEN HEART SURGERY

I watched while one man's heart filled the hand
of another. I noted the inviolate pulsing
envied the sheer tenacity.
We stood like a green sea at the edge of a field

of sterility. The surgeon misbehaved—
became a mad hatter, tossed a dart
at the nurse anesthetist, a dear miss.
It was my job to pour blood through a funnel

to absorb the arterial backlash, become a version
of suicide. The paper sheets rustled
in the clean breeze. We all spoke *sotto voce.*
From the back row, someone sang,

If I give my heart to you.
And all the while, the ghost of Gertrude Stein
was whispering in my ear: *Circle one.*
You were made for something bitter, bitter, better.

IN THIS BUSINESS OF TOUCH
AND BE TOUCHED

It's overdetermined, the body—
a sum of rigid limits. Filament nerves
swan-necked around blunt fingertips.

A dorsal branch
ramified at the tender nail-bed,
every sinew and fiber held at wait and want.

Heart wants out, lungs want air.
They never say enough.
The mouth gives up whatever is formed there—

t's and d's clip the enameled incisors.
The brain, skullbound and wrapped
in spider's web

knows everything about desire.
Knows that what happens happens
to you, for you.

The head is almost an island,
at the outer edge imagined meets real,
silt of one embracing the reef of other.

The test of truth is whether fabric leaves a mark
where skin pressed itself.
Last night, a red wine stain bent the head

of the one who lifted it,
the weaver's grown daughter; her hair kissed
my right hand, a palm full of nerve endings

identical to those that hug the tibia of a rabbit
coat the tongue of a duck.
Across the room, a man's shadow grazed mine.

Scars are formed by such abrasions:
the shrouded want of cheek and shoulder
that arms can't reach, throat refuses to ask.

PUTTING DOWN A CAT

Death is more brutish than I expected.
Was this to whom I sent those love notes
when I was nine?

He hectors the doctor with the blue syringe,
the assistant in white.
His breath is a mix of narcissus

and nightshade; tainted eyes
catch the burnish of fluorescent bulbs.
He's not at all like a father

in sepia photographs: rakish mustache,
pleated wool trousers.
To think I had always imagined him

as someone from nighttime television
who reunites those twins separated at birth
and now forever marred

by what they missed. The cat *is* no longer.
Her body sheds its unused breath;
a muscle twitches in objection.

Nothing now can be undone. Any moment
the door will open; our lives will insist,
then come in.

Death licks the cat's face, smooths her fur,
hands her back—
a hand warmed thing, improbable.

A GODDESS SHAKES SPRING AWAKE

We resemble each other: mischievous
without criminal intent. A hodgepodge of want
to be good but attracted to evil, of guilt

and *Oh, God* to a face that stays hidden.
The quick all share the same air, block the sun
and throw shadow, yet each follows

their own unique blueprint of torment—
some go mad, some rob, all suffer
from flashback and hindsight. You are

like them: both thicket and gift, anguished,
part water. I worry you will be used up.
We are webbed together, an odd apparatus.

Is this what it means to befriend? To speak
with astonishing truth. Awake, you are most
like true worship: unbidden, delirious, and tinged

with the bitter. And not wrong when you state
that death will release you from a terror
of light touch and fever, palm print and flesh.

But death is a river away and this is what
you are good for: fluted field and naked bough
under satellite and sinew of wire.

THE CLAIRVOYANT

Whose face doesn't fall? Cruel mockery
of mask and hide of night clay.

The once-beautiful woman waits
at the window, vaguely tracing

the patterned brocade's jacquard weave.
Who wouldn't rather

recall the lines of a lover's long hair?
I wet the ends with my tongue once.

In Italy, Siena perhaps, I stood in a narrow
stairwell, fear pressed against stone.

Nowhere to go except back.
I felt a man's ribs in their cage.

He didn't mind. If we owe each other
anything, it's a small degree of intimacy.

I've been a coward most of my life,
nothing unusual.

Whoever argues this has never asked
her own heart what it is to be.

I know the truth: my face giving way, lines
becoming furrows in a bed of tilled earth.

I am the earth, *quartz-fret and sparks of salt.*
I will be pressed against. Known.

THE ELEMENTS OF STYLE

First, I'm delicate—
hair a cascade of landscaped curl.
You see

how I love you.
On page forty-five I'm fairer still
dressed in hope-green taffeta

crushed and released.
A mute torrent.
I'm daughter to my own

face on page forty-six:
lovelier in fading.
I will be,

in elegiac black, another *I* caught and held
in place—
trace of pearl circling

a chokered throat
above the single sad ribbon
of later. The end

of eyelid's flutter and fall. Tangled
in grosgrain and difficult.
Beautiful.

WHAT IS RED

Not fire. We stopped to watch one burn,
a two-story frame house on Florissant Road
heir to arson's fuel and rag.

I loved the boy I was with for his lips.
One other night, we swerved
into a gas station's darkened parking lot

now ablaze in squad-car strobe.
A deadly quiet, an open door—
strip of sallow light. I stood in sooty shadow

while he went to look inside. The boy
(his name was Bill) turned back, tight-lipped
face slant and skewed.

You don't want to see, he said.
Timidity aside, I did want
loving everything red: maroon Victoriana,

an open mouth, breast of the robin
in its sad shoe box coffin, mercury's febrile rise,
warm blood of sedition and curious bed.

IN ST. JOHN'S HOSPITAL

My mother and I drifted in a boat
at the edge of the carpet
waiting for some word to come down.

Instead, euphemisms, muffled
hammering, insipid landscapes in peach
and pale.

Outside, red brick divided
the fabric of late spring. A river limped by,
refusing comfort, a cool *mere.*

At home, a shrimp chenille robe,
crumpled gray hat, classic black dress
all leaned toward wear, a whisper

of *done.* Once on a back yard swing
I became the sky I meant to be.
Dead can be anything,

teeth in a glass. Last night, in a dream
we were driving on ice.
He made me get out and sweep . . .

All our lives we carry a condition inside.
Too late we realize—dry sand
dust, what might have been a house.

To be pure, to begin again at zero.

AUTOPSY

How bare the soul—unmasked, deveined,
picked clean. How smooth the flesh
in death. Someone has arrived
to wash the dust away. Mulberry stains.
Indelible marks in hidden places.
Look at you. No longer resisting; unfolding
with ease; revealing scars
from wounds that were slow to heal.
The body remembers. You never won
but dearly battled. The sky here
is streaked with tile.
The scientific community
and the mildly curious have all come
to watch. You bloom in this forest of white.

WHERE SNOW FALLS

Finally, simple
And enough—
Reduced to the instantly
Recognizable—car, curb, dark

Striation of street.
Enviable knickknack planet.
With one glance
The eye takes in the scene: forever

Mitted fingers,
Bright muffled throat, swiss dot
Of shaken snow.
And straight up

That floating slip
Of frigid air
Where colorless sky
Meets cover of glass.

It says,
This world is closed.
No one here is ever lost; nothing
Cannot be won.

IF WISHES WERE HORSES

That the wound had never been
its vast geography, red terrain forming
somewhere near the level of the heart, frayed
edges folding together

like a wake that closes after the departed.
Had it never bled so, a redundant sea
dissolving the side rails
of ships crossing at right angles.

Without the wound, she might have had
the chrome skin of a girl
behind glass, red lips just out of reach.
Yes, energy conserves

itself, but a second time it's useless,
a dull warmth embracing the ceiling's vacancy.
And the between
is but once. In a 9.7 moment of pain

we all become expert, ancient, cousin
to simple persistence. Beggars, prodding
airy nothings, making promises: hay and a bed
in the stable, if only.

ELECTRA DREAMS

Night is when I give you new clothes.
Suits you never owned, borrowed cuff links
rented ties, until you look nothing like
your former self.

The gods might strike me dead if they knew
you were the object of this sad ecstasy.
Sometimes I dress you as the well-dressed man
I pass each morning on the street.

I'm drawn to his brown suede hat.
Or the doctor with soft hands who told me
it's best to think of pain as a number
between one and ten.

You've been many things, all the same.
I've grown to think of you as someone
who keeps calling me back, just
as I'm about to leave. Tonight, you are infant

easy to love. I hum you a tired bit of Brahms
until you're almost asleep, then place you
next to my breast. This is the dream -
swimmer's deep, that unbridled edge

of anarchy, where everything's a pale
blue-green and the air itself is drinkable.
It's safe to speak here.
To call love by a name other than vengeance.

THE CROSSING

You've shadowed me lately, a mixed blessing.
Of course, I don't mind

when you direct the waiter's gaze
to my empty cup, you and I both knowing

what's what. Whistling in the funeral cortege?
No, it wasn't I. I never learned to whistle.

But I sang from my lakeside house. Out of key
and all day: oddments, inimical to sorrow.

Treaties are possible but timing is everything.
I'll take as cue the re-seeded moon,

bulb and blight, a knock (thrice)
with no one behind. The stationmaster calls out

once, twice. O, the bliss of a defined domain.
The platform fills to its fine edge; the train,

a striation of heat. Fruition is a place to go,
a country outside the self—never visited

yet familiar as the first arthritic knuckle
ushering in a new age. Where have you gone?

Now that you've crossed over, can you tell me
What does forgiveness look like? I am waiting

on divined revelations.
The eye will only bring the train this close.

THE HOLY GRAIL

If it were simple, would we have come?
Armored from skull to boot tip
astride a snorting beast.

The morning air is gray with cadaver breath,
pale stink of rotting flesh, the dead
yesterday. When we arrived

this littered hill was clean.
And those we came to fight, to tame
had everything—so it seemed.

In the alcoves, the reliefs
have missing faces,
entire heads are lost, figures reduced to folds

of robe, scallops of hair. Dust pours
from the Cathedral dome.
Bodies absorb the damp ricochet

of a pigeon trapped against glass.

PERSEPHONE LEAVING

She's picking flowers, meadow goldenrod
and belladonna, sometime near noon.
Do you see her? Hugging the shade

at the meadow's edge. And comes Pluto
from Hades in his golden chariot
heart full of flung arrows from cupid's bow.

Sees her and knows for certain *this one,*
her, Persephone but can't say why.
It only takes a single *Trust me*

and she climbs inside. She would kiss him
but he says, *It isn't done*
like that where I come from. And who to know

better than a man with many names.
Black horses paw the ground impatient
and it begins to rain, so they leave.

In Hades she is Queen. Her subjects, shadows.
She doesn't mind: so much the better,
they don't talk back.

She cries, but only later—when she has to leave,
retract her adoration from him
at the door, temple statue with gleaming feet

where hands have enacted a litany of touch.
And he? He feels an arrow break free:
a brief moment of difficulty

as it navigates an arterial narrowing.
She had wanted to eat the whole fruit.
Knowing there would be hell to pay upstairs,

he stopped her. Heart-sick, she refuses
to look at him—seven pomegranate seeds clutched
in her hand and the always ravenous hunger.

BEHIND THIS PASSION

Through small but audacious acts of theft
the *I* becomes a self. In-grain and esoteric
the face gets tucked away

in a blurred photograph of a half-sister;
concealed in a mother's marriage license,
stale sandwich of signatures

wrapped by red borders. The roots
of possession turn to evidence—a chest
of burled veneer, twice injured

by the once-loved; a stranger's police file
detritus bought for a dollar
in a second-hand store. It's stamped:

Parole Violation. An unsmiling accused
(still beautiful) wears a strand of pearls—
front and side views—each bead, the hour

that was owned for a while. *Sentenced
to 20 years for Murder in the 2nd degree,
Jefferson County, Alabama.*

This too has ended. *1925. Female.
Hair, brown; Teeth, good.* The wounding
description: *scar above the left elbow.*

Her inked prints
course the ragged card stock, become
a noisy Rorschach, dark mirror facing out.

WHAT WAS SEEN

Who wouldn't have grown into longing?
Summer's fretwork of mosquito and fireflies mocking

the false alchemy of ever and elsewhere—the wish to be
where we weren't—a wall rose

clinging to a trellis. When Eddie Marten kissed me
in the afternoon, he smelled of thick soup and cigarettes.

An Emerson fan scanned the room corner to corner.
Goodbye Henrietta. Goodbye Camille.

Chalk nights and the dream of heat relieved
by dueful thunder, wind so fierce

it would blow the raindrops sideways.
Whim and nimble impulse. Fat rats in the gully

scattered by a shotgun's kangaroo. Two murders
in the store at the top of the hill in March.

The knife never seen but called by the mind
enormous horror, brigand slaughter. The end. The end.

METAPHOR AS SYMPTOM
OF REASON'S DESPAIR

I took the bus home just to be near a neighborhood:
clothes on the line, the wings of a red blouse,

sail of warm March. A two-story house—
patio and lamppost, bald man in dark green

clipping a ledge. Roof is illusion; house is illusion.
The sky is a palate, blue tears.

Winter's topiary—still empty, outstretched. Yes, yes,
of course the sky is also a turned cup over barbed wire

and heart break. Fossils remain in Cambrian shale:
the body as mouth, gut and bone.

An uncommon efficiency, tentacled, spineless.
Is this living? The white moorland horse seen running

in snow, impelled by a grammar that cannot be heard.
Fog on the car window, veil over nothing at all.

NONESUCH

It's meaning we're looking for:
the jewel shudders
in January harsh light;

a ball bounces; the crowd predicts
its own future. Watch the magician
he's suited and worthy.

Artlessly, he inserts his tin sword—
a bluff, yes. But we close our eyes
to disbelief. We are damaged,

enraptured. His influence outlives
the performance—
a blood orange at breakfast

and it all comes back: the sword,
the love of miracles. Only parade
and circus achieve the nonesuch

we hope for. All other routes
are sown with burdock,
desertthorn, nests of catbrier

with tiny curved bristle. Of course
there is a garden under this one,
a lover there of whom you're sure.

THE FALL

What brought me here to walk a room's periphery
touch each object, as if for luck—

the table's vinyl cloth, embossed, the chairs,
slender shards of aloe

escaping a clay pot? What do you think of the paint
by number scene: horse and rider, air beneath their feet?

At the organ a man is playing *Nearer My God, To Thee.*
His shoes are clean, as if he walked on water—

a roiling sea. He is my father. The air holds
disturbs nothing. No one wakes here.

In some countries, the left hand is unclean, the sole
must never be shown. The underside of my shoe says

Italy, and I think of the clock tower in Siena,
of one who threw himself. I have known

people who died violently—in a car
thrown from a mountain road in Colorado.

If only the terror of the next step
were not so absorbing, we might see more. Falling

is remarkable. Just this afternoon,
in a hurrying crowd, a man fell at my feet

his head lay on the ground—lapdog, homunculus,
sad thing. Once on a swing, I fell from standing,

my slick shoes facing out, hands slithering
over coarse rope, sky becoming earth and blister.

To have come so far.
The room is finished, everything touched.

I'm moving toward the door, curtain of music behind me.
The gun on the wall never fired and this,

the last act. The door opens onto palm and succulents,
bright night of distance. My father continues to play

although I am paradise leaving him.

NO TALKING

No talking in the grass, only persistent scars
where cheek lay to hear
a sound: the distilled conversation

of minute barbed legs, fiddle bow to fiddle.
No movement on the pond surface—
water slurring its beaded lining, blunted tapestry

of black and blacker, brown and tan. No talking
on the part of two dogs engaged
in chase and turn, alike under coats

wet dun and spotted damp, the heart's steady
hiccough under layers of fascia, muscle, rib.
Hands spill the pond water. Nothing can be grasped.

Why indelible hunger? Why insatiable need?

IV

SLOW DANCER

These are difficult times. Your beloved won't speak
only points out what is missing—
that piece of brickish-red could be the edge
of a building, the gossamer blue might be the sky.

It's Tuesday, the oracle of stone.
It may cheer you to know there's a song now
for every occasion. The comfort of a doorway
demands requiem or fugue; a dirge can be found

in the light shade of gray where two shadows meet.
One day you'll be grateful
that music's been written especially for this.
Over time, you'll be expert—high-pitched, lean.

You'd like to know more but the clairvoyant
is so rarely at home—or demands more
than you have now in pocket or purse.
Be careful of twice-folded notes:

inevitably they say, *Warning: You have no future.*
If Madame's not in, tell them you'll be back
after supper, a quick sip of tea. Leave your name,
a number where you can surely be reached.

Beg them to call. You know how to receive.
After all, you learned echoes from emptiness
tapping from canes. Wait to be summoned
from a field where mist curls your hair

where yellow leaves fall, thin-veined and glorious.
Watch the dog who can't see walk toward and away;
dance with someone who calls himself *Sadness.*
When night arrives soundless—nestle against him.

ASHES

Under snow, the park is monotone.
Cat stripes band a mound of dirt.
The problem is description: it falls flat
when distance is the fixed abyss.

Wish you were here is a hollow rejoindure.
In the absence of touch—sight
and sound can compensate only for so long.
One bus passes another, offers faces

framed in black glass. A museum stands
at the corner, a terminus.
When the living carry the dead
into a next world, it's best if they go in a box.

Ashes: urn. Sarcophagus: worm. Marble
isn't so much carved as chiselled away.
Each of these buildings
began as a hollowing: after one thousand

and one nights, Shahrazad allowed the story
to end. She was tired of talking, she said,
and had seen the light—
if he didn't love her by now, he never would.

LIKE SPIDERS, STEP BY STEP

We're moving Duchess, or so it seems.
From the train window, we catch sight
of a moldering castle:
what used to be moat, is nothing but frogland
near the edge of a river.

You know how it happens: train tremor
and two metal bars are speeding you past
let be and *bygone*. Someone you love
is right there beside you,
spine snug to the plush of the seat.

Then without warning—a humdudgeon
or flutter. You open your eyes
and the one who was there turns to wave—
wind blown hair, wild-eyed—
from the back of a rabbit, or rises in the hiss

of a sparrow hawk's wings.
The train doesn't stop.
No instrument registers the ache of the act.
Only now there goes missing
that delicate issue of mortal and mind.

You travel on, headed somewhere yourself:
where house, where dog.
Where a thin layer of glitter
covers years of shamed wear
and loss is now what you live with.

& THERE HE KEPT HER, VERY WELL

Harsh orange, dull burn
of realization.
My imperfections, once subtle,

are now inadmissible.
Still he keeps me
like a pretty need-not

in this fusty dungeon.
Someone has chosen poorly:
a pale persimmon for the walls,

the ceiling, the floor.
A single window, no door.
Hands dip into the vat,

a vicarage of strings.
He's removing the seeds
installing them in egg cups.

Soon a tray of tender shoots
will phosphoresce
in the dark. He wants me

to brighten
says a well-lit face will dazzle.
Outside, the dogs

have begun to howl.
Look—
it's Hecate, a torch in each hand.

RENUNCIATION OF DREAMS
AND SUCH

The night you wandered in the wrong direction
and woke up among strange bedfellows
odd man out in houndstooth blazer

and khaki pants, you called me for advice
but I had none to give.
That night I dreamed: a shower, a rat, an idle knife.

There is no sense subjecting dreams to light:
the truth is, they live underwater and even there
give only a passing glimpse of what we need.

Last night, I dreamed of macaroons,
those small delectables. I tried one
but found it overmuch, returned it to its silver plate

where a rim of tortured dogwood,
branch and unfelled bloom, held the cakes in place.
I once loved a man

who studied the quiet splendor of cut glass
tinted pink with rosé, amber with Grand Marnier.
In those days, I didn't dream.

Not even the night a hurricane unsuckled trees
and laid them side by side.
January that year began and ended as a wave

of gray intensity that converted the world to ice
and froze water where it hid behind the wall.
In the realm of *hard, cold* and *done for,*

it's best to rely on nothing but touch
and temperature—in a system where *zero* stands
for the treason of warmth.

HOW TO LEAVE A PRAIRIE

Don't worry, the Moon will rise
wherever you go. It does even here

miles away from the land's monopoly
of red barns and bent grasses.

My own ancestors lumbered across
in ox carts, passing down a strange tendency

to buy mislabeled maps.
Of course, what each new generation

has to learn for itself is the art
of light packing, weight of a detail,

the patient watch for the Sun's eclipse.
You've seen a lunar shadow

slash Earth's surface at the speed
of a thousand miles per hour,

moving west to east, darkening small towns
with flat names: *Rantoul, Monee,*

a misplaced *Manhattan.* Now let the door
of a white house slam shut; abandon

lawn orb and tractor. Let a woman sob
at a window—silhouetted, otherworldly.

FROM A NEW PLACE

I'll go to Santiago in a coach of black water
—Federico García Lorca

In answer to your question: Yes,
time does go faster here. The light
above the Hudson changes with scintillating speed.
Such a display, I've been told, can cause seizures
in the susceptible few. Dogs do well, however,
chasing their own fitful shadows and squirrels
quickly learn to sit open-mouthed
beneath a tree while November shakes acorns
and the season earns its name.

With cats, it's a different story. My own Emily
has found a suitcase which smells of the place
we most recently left. She's wrapped herself
around it, waiting to be returned.
Each morning, I check the mirror
to assure myself it's not I who languishes there.
Thank you for the quote from Lorca.
We have those same black water coaches here.
                    When it rains,

the herringbone pattern of the red brick path
disappears, distorting all rightful sense of space.
This can lead to confusion.
Just yesterday, I wrongly connected two people
in a laundromat—a man reading a newspaper
and a woman folding clothes.
I myself avoid the washers with the small windows,
wanting no one here
to see the worn, the ragged, the missing.

60

BARTÓK IN THE SCULPTURE GARDEN

String Quartet No. 4 (1928)

Bows like swords impaling air, lit windows
scaling distant buildings—boxcars
into   darkness.
Could I have dreamed twin beds?

Lacquered black, leafed with gold.
The steadfast, the utterly changed, the never
been better, each turning into
the antecedent of a foreign *now*.

The violinist's straight hair curls
in the night's humid air; the cellist's head
hardly moves, her arm   a wing.
A fourth is hidden by a torso in bronze.

Nothing intertwines until lightning
shears the sky into deckled-edge unequals.
Sudden dart of dead-bolt thunder:
I did love him once. Fourteen. He was tall and shy.

Buildings surround, flaunt stores of familiar:
Chippendale & five-colored chintz.
The pleasure of dissonance
is lack

of resolution; fugitive logic, as in:
There are no accidents, only two fates—there
& there. *It was January,*
famous for beginnings: broken pipes

& water cascade. The relief of giving in
to destruction.
In the game of Idiot's Delight,
the skirted queen becomes an infanta cosmos—

her pinched waist
dissolves in a bell-shaped curve
that unfolds on either side into corridors:
one lined with glittering gold, the other, sinister

melodic madness
& both, the gift of god
and goddess grown mortal & blind.
The only constant is replacement & understudy,

substitution & gone:
the flickering kiss—delicate, unutterable.
The musicians bow, strings still vibrating,
unfulfilled, final notes hovering

under swollen canopy:
black leaf, ragged sapphire. They bow
a second time—four metronomes—& gash
the night.

REIGN OF UNREASON

The year's end: a period
of revelry, abrogation of time, the cleansing
that closes the winter.

The snake has all but shed its skin,
nothing remains but hollow quotations.
Tonight we'll send two away—malice and evil

tied to the back of whichever goat
or goose has drawn that lot.
Kata and *strophein*

crouch behind hazed yellow smoke.
We are best when we're mortal and doomed.
We hang figs round their necks,

a dark string for him, white string for her.
Give each a loaf of barley bread, some cheese.
Then we strike them

with squills—sea onion, lily hyacinth—
and branches cut from the Chaste-tree.
Out with hunger.

In with Health and Wealth.
Someone plays, violin or accordion,
I can't tell which. The slow-dying inn keeper

picks me up, twirls me in a half-dance
stranding me between heaven and earth.
Out with hunger.

The door is open: yellow fog and night
tears glisten above fists with clenched stones.
Be thou our offscouring.

Tomorrow—nothing but new. We'll burn
the garments they wore, fripperies of holly bough.
How fortunate we'll be then, how purely defined.

USES OF RESTRAINT

The porch is gray—midway between *flint*
and *whale*—the house, a facade of late sun.

Two women sit outside in June
of a memorable year while a child sleeps

just inside an open door. *Note:*
Keep description to a minimum.

Avoid adjectives, use adverbs
sparingly. The el train passes, troubling

the windows, revising the sun's even center
until a black band is worn through.

She rises from her chair, disappears
from view. *Never hang a gun on the wall*

in Act I, unless you plan
to have it go off in the last act. She leaves

the child playing in the back yard; the dog,
sighing on a porch; takes the car.

She has studied Russian literature. Now,
she raises the camera to her eye

Story telling is deceptively easy.
Every sentence should address the question,

And then
what happened?

and faces the oncoming
train. Bright pills in her purse, abandoned

ironing board, incomplete shopping list
taped to a white metal door: *Bread,*

Milk. Lamb, with a red line through it.

TWILIGHT AMNESIA

Born of bonehouse and charnel, from *forgive
this disaster,* from one who could no longer be
but left you bereft in a back yard
under apple and leaf.
How do these things happen?

I married your father and you
became child and brother to my own.
A house locked us together, rooms parted
by farcical doors opening
and emptying one into the other,

binding us not by title and birthright
but by twilight
amnesia, that graceful remission
and poignant forgetting: birth pang and labor,
a bitter delivery. We are all born

at least twice: to mother and other.
And things can be borrowed:
gift comes from *geve,* loanword from land
of finger-fringed coast—cold, inhospitable
means act of bounty, new owner:

Thou hase giffene thi part of bothe away.
You were awful but artless, beyond intrigue
and connivance; I was worse
and uncalled for. Each of us cursed
but compelled and comprising—

eventually—mother and son.
Two soft-speaking mirrors, welded together
not by incident or accident
of father and husband but by a cohering
day-in, day-out:

As there is no firme reason to be rendred . . .
So can I give no reason. I do not need
to tell you there is love that outlasts
an untender beginning. I cannot, nor would I
give back what's been given.

CAFÉ EDGAR

It's madness: white peonies, bird of paradise,
dwarf orchid, a ceiling erasing itself,

clock ticking loss in a heart that's been murmured
by fever. This is where you wait

for what will never or for one who has left you
shattered. *Come back. Come back.*

A raven watches from the dark corner.
You order the tomato salad grown from seeds

of optimism. By the door sits a dimpled girl.
Her flowered dress, an echoing note.

In an excess of adjectives, wonderful
will do. Each day is the same, the man

at the far table still finishing his tea, crossing his legs,
lighting a cigarette. Finally he sighs, free now

to read his watch. The world outside is other,
distance is lavish. A barred window

transforms each passerby: segmented thorax,
hunched back, scurrying legs—but no more insect

than you or I. Over shallow soup bowls
we wake to sleep. This is the bread: body, soul,

exquisite tenderness. We are all we have.

NOTES

In Order Not to Be Eten Nor All to Torne
  The title is from a usage example under the word "wolf" in the *Oxford English Dictionary, 2nd Edition.*

The Clairvoyant
  "Quartz-fret and sparks of salt" is taken from a poem by Gerard Manley Hopkins: "With blackness bound, and all / The thick stars round him roll / Flashing like flecks or coal, / Quartz-fret, or sparks of salt, / In grimy vasty vault" ("The Blessed Virgin Compared to the Air We Breathe").

Metaphor as Symptom of Reason's Despair
  References to fossils found in Cambrian shale come from a newspaper article, "Oldest Multicell Organisms Are Reported in Fossil Find," *New York Times,* 4 April 1995.

Ashes
  Rejoindure: a joining again, reunion.

Like Spiders, Step by Step
  The title comes from Aeschylus's play *The Suppliant Maidens* (translated by S. G. Benardete). The maidens are the fifty daughters of King Danaus about to be taken against their will to Egypt to marry their cousins. They speak as a chorus: "Alas, father, to the sea he leads me; / Like a spider, step by step, / A dream, a black dream, / Cry, O woe, cry!"

Bartók in the Sculpture Garden

Idiot's Delight is the game of solitaire. Infanta is an "*adj, of a fashion in dress:* derived from Velasquez's portraits of 17th century princesses and usually having wide skirts with side extensions." *Webster's Third New International Dictionary.*

Reign of Unreason

The poem draws on Sir James Frazer's 1922 classic study of mythologies, *The Golden Bough,* especially those sections dealing with the public expulsion of evils and the practice of scapegoating. *Kata* (down) and *strophein* (turned) combine to form the Greek word *katastrophe* (an overturning), from which the English word "catastrophe" derives.

Twilight Amnesia

Italicized lines represent usage examples for the word "give" in the *Oxford English Dictionary, 2nd Edition.* The spellings in "As there is no firme reason . . ." (from Shakespeare's *The Merchant of Venice* iv.i.59) have been changed slightly to conform to spellings found in an earlier folio than the one quoted in the *OED.*

Café Edgar

In the latter half of 1844, Edgar Allen Poe finished writing "The Raven" at a farmhouse located near this café on West 84th Street in Manhattan.

About the Author

Mary Jo Bang grew up in St. Louis and was educated at Northwestern University, Westminster University (London), and Columbia University. Her poems have appeared in *Colorado Review, Denver Quarterly, New American Writing, The Paris Review, Partisan Review,* and elsewhere. In 1995, she received a "Discovery"/*The Nation* award. She lives in Manhattan.

University Press of New England publishes books under its own imprint and is the publisher for Brandeis University Press, Dartmouth College, Middlebury College Press, University of New Hampshire, Tufts University, and Wesleyan University Press.

Library of Congress Cataloging-in-Publication Data
Bang, Mary Jo.
   Apology for want / Mary Jo Bang.
     p. cm.
   ISBN 0–87451–821–0 (alk. paper). — ISBN 0–87451–822–9 (pbk. : alk paper)
   I. Title.
PS3552.A47546A84   1997   97–1760
811'.54—dc21